Plantilles:
Plants of St. Martin

Part One: Native Plants on St. Martin
Part Two: Agricultural Roots on St. Martin
Part Three: Bush Medicine on St. Martin
Part Four: Plants and Traditions on St. Martin
Part Five: Flowers at The Old House

By Mark Yokoyama

Part One: Native Plants on St. Martin

The Tree of Life, Plants to the Rescue and
Made for Island Life: Survival Superpowers of Native Plants

THE TREE OF LIFE
Our endangered native treasure

The Gaïac or Lignum Vitae (*Guaiacum officinale*) is native to the Caribbean. It is a slow-growing tree that was once common in the region but is now endangered due to centuries of overharvesting for its wood, the hardest in the world. Much of the wood was exported for shipbuilding and other purposes. Locally, it was historically used for mortars, like those made for pounding arrowroot. The sap or resin of the tree was also thought to have medicinal properties–for this reason the Gaïac has been called the Tree of Life.

The Gaïac tree has a dense crown, and it is one of the few trees that manages to stay green during dry periods and droughts.

The trees are capable of growing over 12 meters tall, and some reports indicate they can live for up to 1,000 years. However, Gaïac is often thought of as a small species because so few large, old trees remain.

The Gaïac has beautiful blue flowers and colorful orange fruit and seeds encased in a bright red covering. Its branches are typically twisted and forked, creating a dense crown. Like other native trees, it provides shelter and food for a variety of local animals, from insects to birds. By planting this tree, we create habitat for native animals even in our own backyards, and help restore this heritage tree for future generations.

The Gaïac has beautiful blue flowers. When it is in bloom, the whole tree explodes into blue.

Gaïac flowers are an important source of nectar for butterflies and other insects.

The Gaïac fruit is bright orange. It opens up to reveal the seed, covered in a bright red coating. A mature tree can produce tens of thousands of fruit and seeds in a year.

Gaïac seeds sprout into seedlings quickly, but the trees grow very slowly. It can take several hundred years for these trees to achieve their full size.

Beneath the bright orange coating, Gaïac seeds are black and hard. They evolved to survive the trip through the digestive system of birds.

The caterpillar of a moth called the Bewitching Melipotis likes to eat Gaïac leaves. It avoids being eaten by birds or lizards by hiding under the loose bark of the tree.

Gaïac illustration by Étienne Denisse, 1846.

PLANTS TO THE RESCUE
Restoring habitat on St. Martin

St. Martin is home to a unique group of plants and animals. There's no place quite like it anywhere else in the world. It is also the most densely populated island in the Caribbean. All our unique nature has to share this small island with lots of people. The wild spaces that we still have are very important.

Healthy habitats, like the tropical dry forest found on many hills, are crucial to local wildlife. As coastlines and lowlands fill up with buildings, diverse hillside habitats are more important than ever.

Hurricanes can cause massive damage to trees and plants. Although native species are adapted to recover, it can be harder when habitats are already damaged by human activity.

Hurricane Irma taught us that both people and nature are at risk on St. Martin. To recover, we need to rebuild. We also need to make sure our wild spaces are healthy. They protect us from flooding and landslides. They keep our beaches and shores from washing into the sea. They keep our island beautiful.

Native trees and plants are the key to healthy habitats. They are adapted to our climate, and they are good at surviving big storms. They provide food and shelter for native animals. Some have specific roles: mangroves protect coastlines and help keep our seas clean.

At Amuseum Naturalis, we are growing native trees and plants for wild spaces, and also backyards and neighborhoods. Native plants are a better choice than exotic species or imported plants that may come with unwanted pests. Landscaping with local species is the perfect way to help local birds and other native wildlife.

Making nature strong makes St. Martin strong. The deep roots of native plants are the foundation of our future.

Native trees like the endangered Lignum Vitae are good at surviving storms and droughts. They are a crucial resource for native animals during hard times.

Mangrove trees have died around many of St. Martin's ponds. Multiple factors may be to blame: drought, pollution and invasive Green Iguanas. Replanting mangroves is a key part of restoring wetlands.

In recent years, unusually dry weather and drought have been common on St. Martin. Climate models predict a drier future for the island. Luckily, many native trees can survive droughts.

Environmental Protection in the Caribbean and the St. Maarten Nature Foundation planted 300 mangrove trees on Little Key in the Simpson Bay Lagoon. Mangroves provide habitat for many animals and protect young fish before they head out to sea.

Rat Apple illustration by Nikolaus Joseph Jacquin.

MADE FOR ISLAND LIFE
Survival superpowers of native plants

St. Martin is a tropical paradise. It's warm and sunny all year, with beautiful blue seas and cool flowing breezes. But paradise is more complicated than it looks for plants and trees. The ones that live here all have special traits that help them survive.

The Sea Grape (Coccoloba uvifera) is extremely good at beach living. It sends out a deep network of roots that holds the tree in the sand and also helps keep the sand on the beach. It is loved for the shade it provides and the plentiful fruit female trees produce. Male Sea Grape trees don't bear fruit, but are needed to pollinate the flowers of the female trees.

Even though it doesn't get cold on St. Martin, there are different seasons here. In general, the fall is a wet season and the spring is a dry season. The dry season pushes plants to their limit. Many lose their leaves to save water. Cacti don't have leaves at all. Other plants hold water in their trunk or send deep roots to find hidden water underground.

The sea and wind can also make life hard for plants. Plants that can live near the coast are ones that can handle salt water or salty sea spray. They can also hold their ground in sandy soil. These special plants get the beach all to themselves, and they protect the island from washing away into the sea.

Plants on St. Martin also need to survive extreme storms. Palm trees are amazingly flexible in strong winds. Other trees lose their smaller branches in a hurricane, but leave their trunk rooted in the ground so they can recover.

On St. Martin, every native plant has adapted to survive drought under the burning tropical sun and the devastation of immense storms. Their adaptations keep St. Martin green.

The Red Mangrove (Rhizophora mangle) is one of the most amazing trees on earth. It lives on the edge of land and water, on coastlines and around ponds. Unlike most plants, it can live with its roots submerged in salt water. These roots trap nutrients before they flow out to sea, protecting coral reefs. Red Mangroves also absorb the energy of waves and storm surge, preventing erosion. Countless birds, fish, crabs and other animals depend on this tree and the habitat it creates. (Illustration by F. Legendre, 1834)

The Gumbo-Limbo (Bursera simaruba) is also known as the Tourist Tree because it has red, peeling bark that looks like a bad sunburn. This tree is very good at surviving hurricanes. All the smaller branches break off, leaving the trunk intact. The fallen branches can even grow into new trees if they land in suitable soil. (Illustration by Jean Théodore Descourtilz, 1822)

The Calabash tree (Crescentia cujete) is known for its fruit, which has a hard shell that is used for cups, bowls and water jugs. It shares its name with the calabash gourd grown in Africa. The two plants are not related, but their dry fruit is used in the same way. Calabash trees grow a few long whip-like branches instead of forking into smaller branches and twigs. Leaves, flowers and fruit grow directly off these main branches. These trees seem to survive hurricanes well, perhaps because the wind can pass right through their open crowns. (Illustration by Dorothy Hall Horsfall, 1835)

The Jamaican Caper (Quadrella cynophallophora) can handle sun, drought and even some salty wind. It uses these talents to live in coastal and dry scrub areas throughout the Caribbean. It usually has a tall, thin shape. Having branches and leaves clustered closely together helps it save water. It's one of the few trees that usually stays green even in the driest times. Its leaves are food for butterflies like the Florida White and Great Southern White. (Illustration by Jean Théodore Descourtilz, 1827)

The Bread 'n Cheese bush (Pithecellobium unguis-cati) often grows in sandy or rocky areas where larger trees can't grow. To help it grow in poor soil, bacteria in its roots take nitrogen from the air and change it to a form the plant can use. Bread 'n Cheese is also called Cat's Claw because it's covered in thorns. Plants growing in these dry and difficult places often have thorns to protect their precious leaves. Caterpillars of a tiny butterfly called the Cassius Blue eat the leaves of this bush. In some places, its bark is used to treat fever and its seeds are used in crafts.

The Rat Apple (Morisonia americana) is a small tree that is common in coastal scrub areas of St. Martin. It is a host plant for the caterpillar of the Great Southern White, a white and yellow butterfly that is very common on the island. The Rat Apple gets its name from its fruit. Fuzzy, round and very hard, they are white on the inside. Although they are apparently edible, the fruit are undesireable: an "apple" that only a rat would eat.

The Doodle Doo cactus (Pilosocereus royenii) grows to the size of a tree, even in the driest parts of St. Martin. It's only found from Puerto Rico through the Lesser Antilles, and it's well adapted to life here. Its roots spread wide and shallow, ready to collect water from even a light rain. Its body holds water and converts sunlight to food, so it doesn't need leaves. It makes flowers and fruit throughout the year, providing food to insects and birds even in dry times when other food is scarce.

The Jumping Prickly Pear (Opuntia triacantha) is a little cactus that is great at living where few other plants can survive. You can find it on stone walls and windswept seaside cliffs. But it doesn't grow very fast. In areas with good soil and water, it will quickly be overgrown by grass and other plants. Although it makes flowers and fruit, this cactus is mostly spread by animals. The spines hook into a passing animal and a segment of the stem breaks off. If the cactus is lucky, the segment falls off the animal in a good spot and it grows into a new plant. (Illustration by Mary Emily Eaton, 1913)

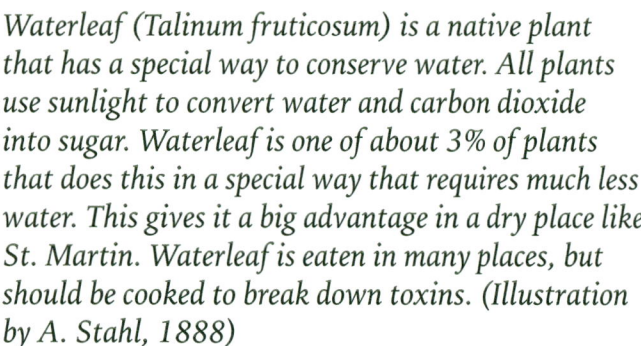

Waterleaf (Talinum fruticosum) is a native plant that has a special way to conserve water. All plants use sunlight to convert water and carbon dioxide into sugar. Waterleaf is one of about 3% of plants that does this in a special way that requires much less water. This gives it a big advantage in a dry place like St. Martin. Waterleaf is eaten in many places, but should be cooked to break down toxins. (Illustration by A. Stahl, 1888)

The West Indian Cherry (Malpighia emarginata) is often simply called Cherry. This delicious fruit is loved by many on St. Martin. It is very high in vitamin C, and varies from sweet to a bit sour. It can be eaten raw, but it's often made into juice or jam. Many of these trees are found around The Old House in French Quarter and down towards the Orient Bay salt pond and Galion Beach. This is an area where many people came to pick cherries in years gone by. (Illustration by A. Stahl, 1888)

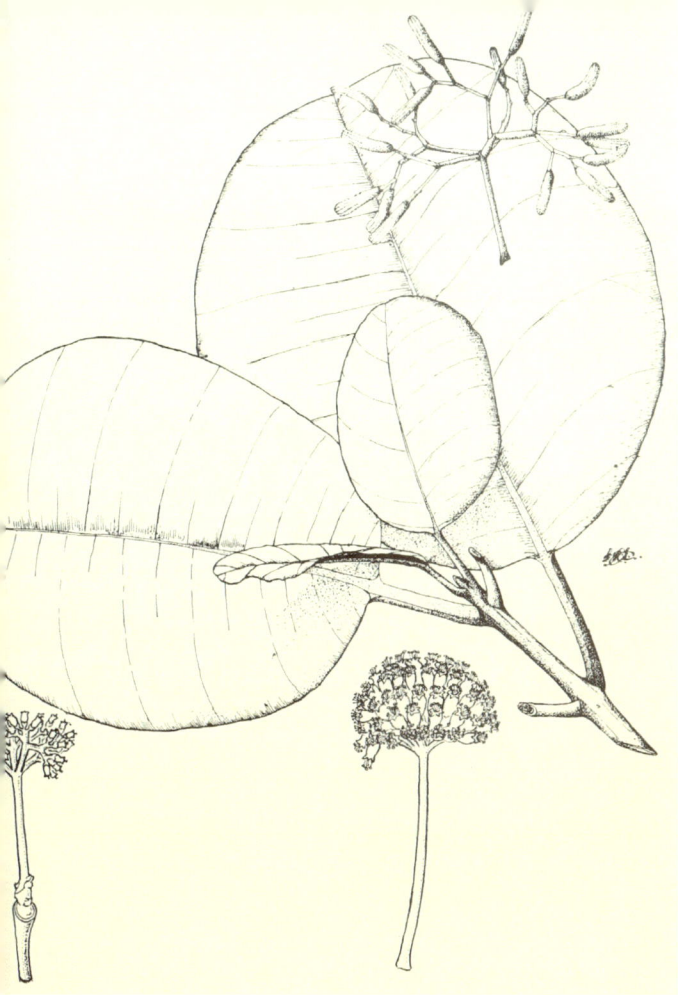

Many of the trees that grow in the dry parts of St. Martin have very hard wood. The Black Loblolly (Pisonia subcordata) is just the opposite. It has a very thick trunk made of soft wood. Soft wood can hold more water, so the trunk of this tree is like a built-in water tank that can keep the tree alive during dry times. Its wood is too soft to use in construction, but because of its light weight, it was traditionally used to make floats for fishing nets.

Also known as the Wild Banyan, the Shortleaf Fig tree (Ficus citrifolia) usually starts its life atop another tree. As it grows, it drops roots to the ground and strangles the tree it is growing on. Although it takes the life of its host tree, it gives life to many animals. Each species of fig is pollinated by just one species of wasp. To make sure its wasp survives, the fig must produce fruit throughout the year. Many animals—like bats, birds and insects—depend on figs at times of year when no other fruits are available.

Part Two: Agricultural Roots on St. Martin

FRUITS OF THE LAND
Original flavors of St. Martin

The first foods on St. Martin were here long before the first people. Many different native fruits were already part of the landscape when the first people came. Before the first people, these fruits were food for native birds and other animals. We can thank the birds for eating these fruits and then spreading the seeds from island to island.

Above: Guava (Psidium guajava) painted by Marianne North in Jamaica, 1872.

The Coco Plum (Chrysobalanus icaco) is seen here with the White-crowned Pigeon (Patagioenas leucocephala), a Caribbean bird that eats the fruit and spreads the seeds of many native trees. (Illustration by Mark Catesby)

Sea Grape (*Coccoloba uvifera*) and Coco Plum (*Chrysobalanus icaco*) are often found near the sea, and still grow wild near many of our beaches. Guava (*Psidium guajava*) and Guavaberry (*Myrciaria floribunda*) do well in valleys with rich soil and plenty of water. Soursop (*Annona muricata*) and Sugar Apple (*Annona squamosa*) were once planted in every backyard.

Today, some native fruits, like the Water Lemon (*Passiflora laurifolia*), are rarely seen. Sea Grapes are still loved for their shade and beauty, but not everyone knows of their delicious fruit. Over the years, many new, non-native fruits like mango, banana and kinnip

The Sugar Apple (Annona squamosa) is also called Sweet Sop and Custard Apple.

became local favorites after they were brought to St. Martin from other parts of the world. Other native fruits still have a strong place in local diet and culture. Guavaberry is a favorite flavor for rum, jam and tarts eaten at Christmas time. Soursop trees are still found beside many houses. Their fruit are enjoyed as juice, smoothies or sorbet and their leaves are used as a bush tea.

The Sea Grape (Coccoloba uvifera) is a popular seaside tree that is used today for shade. Its fruit is loved by some, but perhaps not as much as in the past.

Soursop (Annona muricata) gets its name from the sweet and sour taste of its fruit. The fruit is loved throughout the Caribbean and has also been brought to Asia and Africa. On St. Martin, the fruit and its juice are both popular. Soursop is also used as bush medicine. The fruit and leaves are used to treat dozens of conditions, from fever to bedwetting. On St. Martin, tea made from a few Soursop leaves steeped in boiled water is taken before bed for better sleep. (Illustration by Berthe Hoola van Nooten)

The Water Lemon (Passiflora laurifolia) is a close relative of the Passion Fruit (Passiflora edulis). Both plants are vines with beautiful flowers. The fruit of the Water Lemon is oval-shaped, and soft and fuzzy on the outside. Inside, the fruit looks like a Passion Fruit, with edible seeds in sweet, juicy pulp. Though delicious, they are not widely grown. Leaves of the Water Lemon are eaten by caterpillars of the Gulf Fritillary (Agraulis vanillae), a medium-sized, bright orange butterfly. (Illustration by Maria Sibylla Merian)

AMERINDIAN GARDENS
The roots of Caribbean farming

Amerindian people brought a variety of food crops to the Caribbean. Some of them have been grown on the islands for thousands of years. These crops are not as familiar as export crops like sugar or cotton, but they have fed countless generations of Caribbean people.

Above: Pumpkin (Cucurbita moschata), painted by an unknown illustrator.

Sweet potato (Ipomoea batatas), painted by an unknown illustrator in 1846.

Cassava was the main crop for Amerindians in the Caribbean. It is a root vegetable from South America, and it has several features that make it valuable here. It is a very reliable crop that can produce food even in poor soil or drought. Once planted, it can grow without additional care. Bitter Cassava is high in cyanide and must be prepared carefully, but also resists pests. Cassava bread can stay good for months.

Many other important Amerindian crops were root vegetables, like Sweet Potato, Tannia and Arrowroot. Root vegetables can be left in the ground and harvested when needed. This is life-saving in times of drought, or when a hurricane destroys above-ground crops. These roots were often grown in mounds of soil, a practice that is still used today.

Although many new crops arrived during the colonial period, these ancient root crops are still grown throughout the Caribbean. Beans, Pumpkin, Corn and other crops grown by Amerindians are also found in most gardens and farms. To this day, the crops and techniques of Amerindian farmers are still feeding Caribbean people.

Cassava (Manihot esculenta), illustrated by Jean-Theodore Descourtilz in 1827.

Arrowroot (Maranta arundinacea), illustrated by an unknown artist in 1808.

Bananas and plantains are both from the genus Musa. Most bananas and plantains cultivated are from a hybrid known as Musa × paradisiaca.

Tannia (Xanthosoma sagittifolium) is a starchy root vegetable, and its leaves are also edible.

A NEW HOME
African crops in the Caribbean

Caribbean farming is a unique combination of plants and techniques from two main sources: Caribbean Amerindians and Africans. This unique combination of traditions can be found in Caribbean farms and gardens all over the region today.

Above: The Watermelon (Citrullus lanatus) comes from Africa and is still wildly popular all over the world.

Guinea Corn (Sorghum bicolor) can be prepared in many ways. The grains can even be popped like popcorn. Illustrated by Jean-Theodore Descourtilz, 1829.

Under slavery, the language, culture and identity of enslaved Africans were deliberately suppressed. But some food and farming traditions have survived through the ages. In their few free hours, enslaved people farmed provision grounds to feed themselves, and this kept farming traditions alive.

Many key crops were brought from Africa. Guinea Corn, or Sorghum, is an African grain. It grows quickly, even in heat and dry weather. Unlike most grains, it is ideal for St. Martin's climate. It is also easy to raise and prepare.

The Pigeon Pea came from Asia, but was popular in Africa by the time St. Martin was colonized. It also grows easily in dry tropical climates. Using a row of Pigeon Pea bushes to mark the edge of a farm or property is a tradition in both Africa and the Caribbean. You can still see this on St. Martin.

Other African crops were soon growing side-by-side with Amerindian ones: African yams, gourds, peas and melons joined Amerindian sweet potatoes, pumpkins and beans. The African technique of ridging soil and the short-handled hoe from Africa are widely used in the region. To this day, farms and gardens on every island show the combined influence of African and Amerindian farming traditions.

White Yam (Dioscorea cayennensis) from Africa is often grown side by side with Amerindian sweet potatoes.

The Pigeon Pea (Cajanus cajan) is a key part of St. Martin cuisine, particularly rice and peas. The plant is very well adapted to the dry tropical climate of St. Martin and can be seen in many yards and gardens. The peas are often harvested around the end of the year. Originally from Asia, this plant was brought to the Caribbean from Africa. The pigeon pea is also an important ingredient in many Indian dishes.

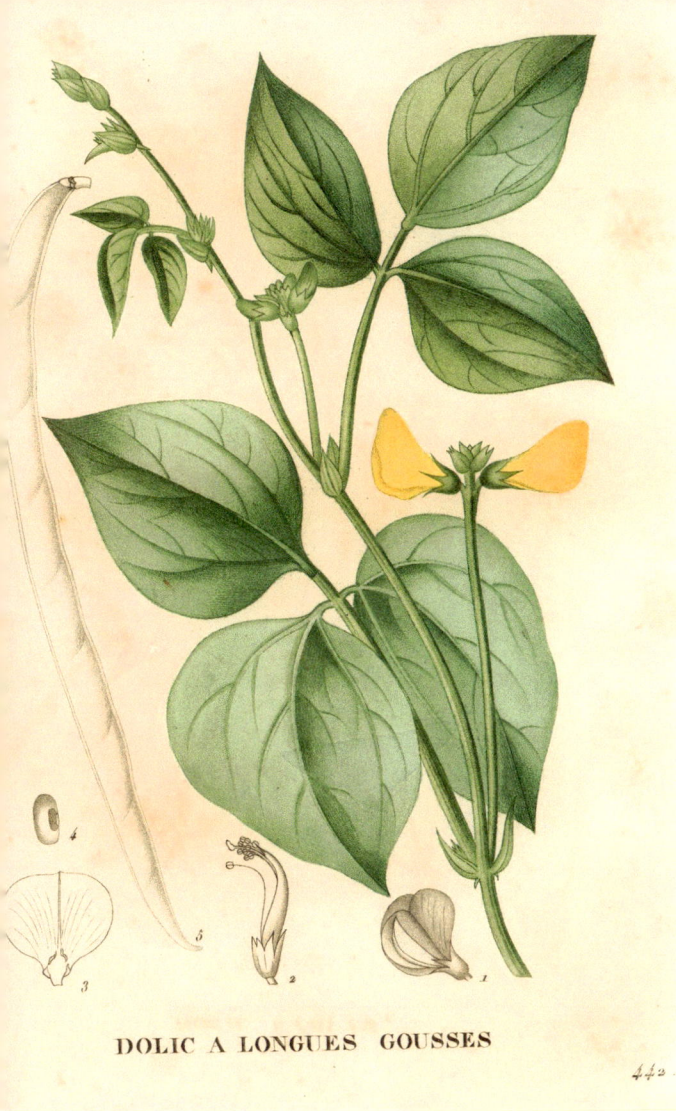

DOLIC A LONGUES GOUSSES
442

Akeesia Africana.

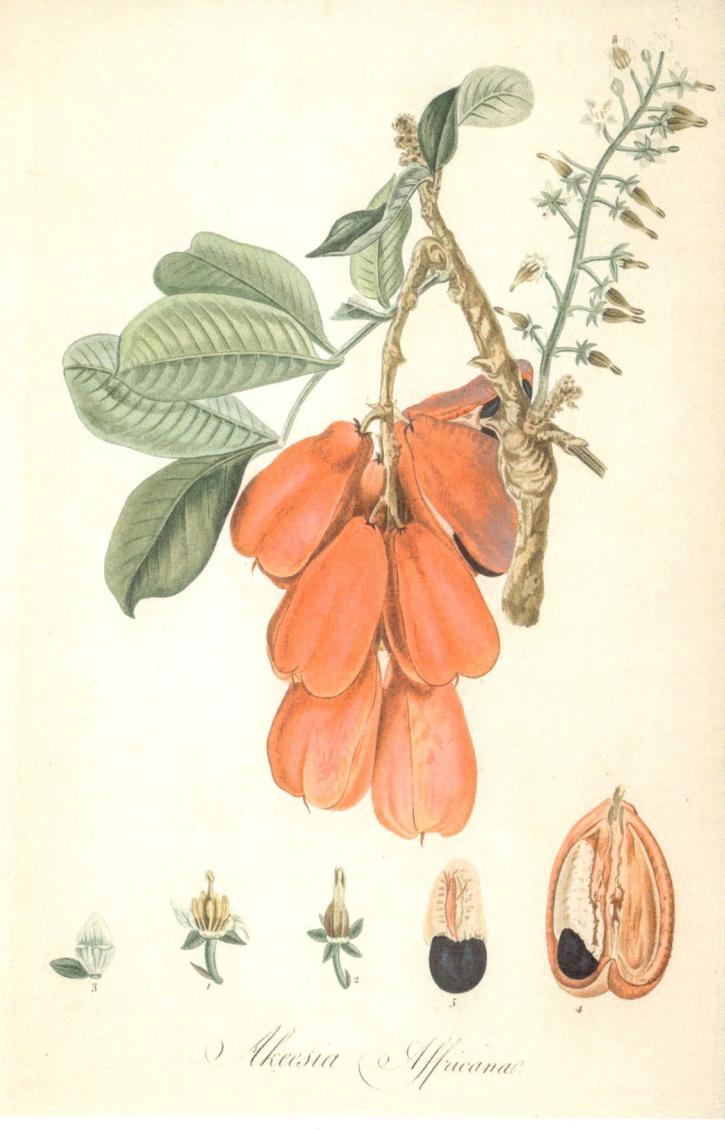

The Cowpea (Vigna unguiculata) was domesticated in Africa and is thought to be one of the world's most ancient crops. It has been bred into many varieties, like the black-eyed pea and yardlong bean.

The Ackee (Blighia sapida) comes from tropical West Africa, where it is called akye fufo in the Akan language. It arrived in the Caribbean in the 1700s, possibly brought across the Atlantic by enslaved Africans. It is particularly popular in Jamaica, where it is the national fruit and part of the national dish: ackee and salt fish. Ackee can only be harvested when the fruits open, because the unripe fruit is very toxic.

Part Three: Bush Medicine on St. Martin

Learn about native plants in bush medicine, African plants and traditions in Caribbean bush medicine and bush medicine in calypso music.

CARIBBEAN HEALING
Local plants in bush medicine

Many local plants are used in bush medicine. How did people learn about them and how to use them? Different groups discovered and shared this knowledge, passing it on through oral tradition.

Amerindians lived in the Caribbean for thousands of years. They knew local plants and how to use them for medicine. Sadly, most of these people were killed by disease or genocide when Europeans arrived. Luckily, they shared what they knew with Africans, who continued to pass it on through the years.

Africans came here with a rich plant medicine tradition. They knew tropical plants and illnesses, but many of the plants here were new to them. They had to develop or adapt plant cures for the Caribbean. By testing plants and techniques, they found treatments. These were passed on orally and refined over time.

Europeans were also interested in plant medicines, especially ones that could be sold to Europe. They mostly relied on Amerindian or Black experts to find plants and explain their use.

Caribbean people continued to refine and share plant cures. A journal found in The Old House recorded the recipe for a plant-based cough remedy from a Pastor Hodge of Anguilla. It noted both the recipe, and that it was effective.

Rat Ears (Peperomia pellucida) is also known as Shining Bush, Inflammation Bush, Information Bush and Watercress. It's used to treat cold, flu and high blood pressure. The leaves are also eaten as salad greens. (Illustration: Jean-Théodore Descourtilz, 1827)

Physic Nut (Jatropha gossypiifolia) is used to clean sores and boils, and to treat constipation. It's also used to treat stomach problems and is called Bellyache Bush in many places. Like many medicinal plants, this plant also contains poisons. Plant healers must know how to avoid poisoning by knowing what parts of a plant to use, how much to use, or how to neutralize or extract poisons. (Illustration: M. Hart, 1823)

Wormgrass (Dysphania ambrosioides) is used to get rid of worms and other parasites. It's used this way in most of the American tropics. This knowledge may have passed through many Amerindian cultures during ancient times.

Canker Berry (Solanum bahamense) is used to treat thrush and sore throat. This plant is closely related to potatoes and tomatoes.

Vervain (Stachytarpheta jamaicensis) is used to relieve menstrual cramps and to treat flu and infection. It's also used to calm nerves. Another name for this plant, Worryvine, may come from this use. Worryvine could also come from the name vervain, which itself comes from the French verveine. Plant names and uses can show that information was shared between islands and cultures.

CURES ACROSS AN OCEAN
A living link to African traditions

Caribbean bush tea and bush medicine traditions have strong African roots. Medicinal and plant skills were carried across an ocean and passed on for hundreds of years. They even survived slavery, which cut ties to African knowledge, cultures and languages.

Africa has one of the world's longest and strongest plant medicine traditions, reaching far back into prehistory. Africans brought plant knowledge, traditions, and plants themselves to the

Caribbean Candlebush (Senna alata) looks like African Candelabra Tree. They have similar uses in both places. They are both used to treat fungal skin infections like ringworm, and candlebush is also called Ringworm Bush. On St. Martin, it is also used to soothe rashes from cement powder and other skin irritations.
(Illlustration: Harriet Thiselton-Dyer, 1879)

Caribbean. Dozens of healing plant species were brought from Africa to the Caribbean during the slave trade. Researchers believe Africans brought these plants because they were the only ones who knew their use.

Africans in the Caribbean also found local plants that were related to ones they used in Africa. Some Caribbean plants are still used here in the same way similar plants are used in Africa today. Some Caribbean plant names seem to come from African plant names.

For most of St. Martin's history, the plant healing based in African and Amerindian traditions was the most effective care around. Even when Western medicine improved on the island, it was out of reach for many because of cost and access. Bush medicine was often still the main care available. Through nonstop use, bush medicine traditions are still alive today on St. Martin and in the region.

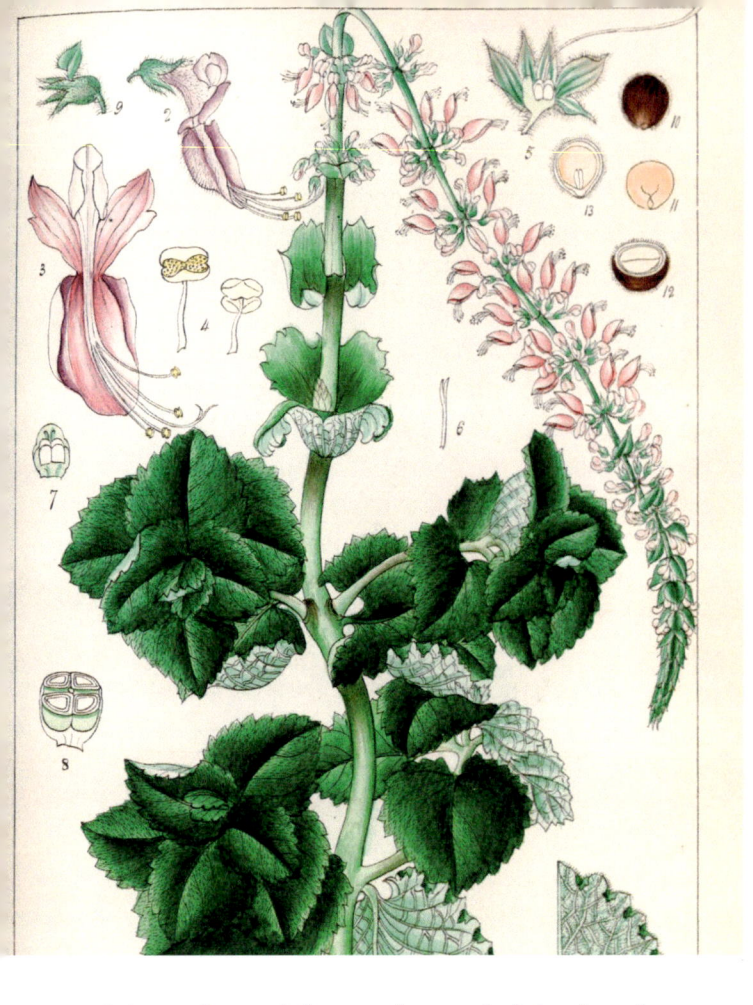

Stingy Thyme (Plectranthus amboinicus) and Paracetamol (Plectranthus caninus) are African plants in the mint family. Both of these plants are found in almost every kitchen garden on the island. They thrive in the local climate and can easily be grown from cuttings. Stingy thyme is often used as a cooking herb, particularly to season fish. It's common in bush tea, often to treat a cough or upset stomach. It's also used to ease morning sickness, to help overdue mothers go into labor, and to boost milk production after childbirth. It's also used on the skin to soothe insect bites. Paracetamol is usually used as a pain reliever. Its local name in both French and English is the name of a commercial pain-relief medicine.

The Jumbie Bead (Abrus precatorius) is deadly. Every part of the plant contains the poison abrin, and a single seed can kill. But it was also used as a medicine and to induce abortion.

Seed Under Leaf (Phyllanthus amarus) is a Caribbean plant that is now widely used in Africa. It also has relatives in Africa that are used as medicine. On St. Martin, it's used for diabetes, fever, high blood pressure, to flush gall stones, and for many other things.

The Maiden Apple (Momordica charantia) was brought to the Caribbean from Africa. It has many uses as food and medicine in both places.

Woman Piaba (Leonurus sibiricus)

WEST INDIAN WEED WOMAN
Plant medicine in calypso music

Calypso music began in Trinidad and became popular throughout the Caribbean. Calypso songs are often funny, and many deal with current events, cultural traditions or everyday life in creative and amusing ways. The song "West Indian Weed Woman" draws humor from the huge assortment of herbal medicines the woman is selling. Over 60 plants and cures are mentioned by name in the version made popular by Guyanese singer Bill Rogers in the 1930s.

This song both draws from and helps preserve Caribbean traditions. The medical knowledge and plant names are Caribbean, making the song topical for Caribbean listeners. It describes a female plant medicine expert. Historically, many skilled healers in the Caribbean were women. The recording itself is a way of documenting important herbal medicine traditions.

Recent analysis of this song found that about 80% of the plants that could be identified are native to the Caribbean. This shows it is likely that Amerindian plant knowledge was adopted by Afro-Caribbean healers, becoming a key part of Caribbean culture to this day.

For more information, read *West Indian Weed Woman: Indigenous Origins of West Indian Folk Medicine* by Erneslyn Velasco and Lawrence Waldron, published in the proceedings of the 27th International Association for Caribbean Archaeology Congress.

Top: Cockshun (*Smilax schomburgkiana*), illustration by F.G. Kohle

Bottom: Wild Daisy (*Sphagneticola trilobata*), illustration by F.W. Horne

West Indian Weed Woman
Recorded by Bill Rogers in 1934

One day I met an old woman selling,
And I wanted something to eat.
I say I was going to put a bit in she way,
But I turn back when I meet.
I thought she had bananas, orange or pear,
But was nothing that I need.
For when I asked the old woman what she was selling, She said she was selling weed.

She had she coat tie up over she waist,
And was stepping along with grace.
She had on an old pair of clogs on her feet,
And was wriggling down the street.
Just then she started to name the different weeds, And I really was more than glad.
But I can't remember all that she call,
But these were a few she had.

Man Piaba, Woman Piaba,
Tantan Fall Back and Lemon Grass,
Minnie Root, Gully Root, Granny-Backbone,
Bitter Tally, Lime Leaf, and Toro,
Coolie Bitters, Karile Bush, Flat o' the Earth, and Iron Weed,
Sweet Broom, Fowl Tongue, Wild Daisy, Sweet Sage and even Toyo.

Top: Toyo (Justicia pectoralis), illustration by L. Bevalet

Bottom: Minnie Root (Ruellia tuberosa), illustration by F.W. Horne

She had Cassava Mumma, Coocoo Piaba,
Jacob's Ladder, and Piti Guano,
Fingle Bush, Job's Tear, Piti Payi, a Jumbie
Bottle, and White Cleary,
Bile Bush, Wild Cane, Duck Weed, Aniseed,
Wara Bitters, and Wild Gray Root.
She even had down to a certain bush Barbajans
does call Puss in Boot.

When I hear how much bush she had,
I left dumb till I couldn't even talk.
She started to call from Camp Street corner,
And never stop 'til she reached Orange Walk.
The woman had me so surprised
that I didn't know what to do,
That a girl come and gimme a cuff in meh eye,
And I didn't even know was who.

Sweet Broom, Sweet Sage, and Lemon Grass, I
hear them good for making tea.
Oh well, I hear Zèb Grass and Wild Daisy
is good to cool the body.
The woman tongue was even lisped,
And she was calling out all the time.
She even had a little kanwa eye,
And the other that left was blind.

Top: Fingle Bush (Clethra alnifolia), illustration by Mark Catesby

Bottom: Sweet Sage (Lantana camara), illustration by D. Bois

She had Bitter Guma, Portugee Bumboh,
Congo Lana, and Twelve o' Clock Broom,
Sarsparilla, Wild Tomato, Soursop Leaf, and
Half-a-bit Weed,
Yura Bally, Sweet Pinpota Bush, White Fleary,
and Christmas Bush,
Cockshun and Sand Bitters, and even Monkey
Ladder, and all the rest you may need.

She had Fat Bush, Elder Bush, Black Pepper
Bush, French Toyo, Qupera, and Capadulla,
Tamarind Leaf, Money Bush, Soldier Fork
Leaf, Pumpkin Blossom, and even Devil Dua,
Leeman, Congo Pom, Pingalor, Physic Nut,
and Lily Root.
In fact, the only bush that she didn't got
was Bush in he everyday suit!

*Lyrics transcription by Erneslyn Velasco
and Lawrence Waldron*

*Top: Fat Bush (Eryngium aquaticum), illustration by
S. Edwards*

Bottom: Devil Dua (Strychnos sp.)

Top Left: Yura Bally (Chelonanthus alatus), illustration by L. Bevalet

Bottom Left: Wild Tomato (Physalis angulata), illustration by M. Blanco

Above: Sweet Broom (Scoparia dulcis), illustration by M. Blanco

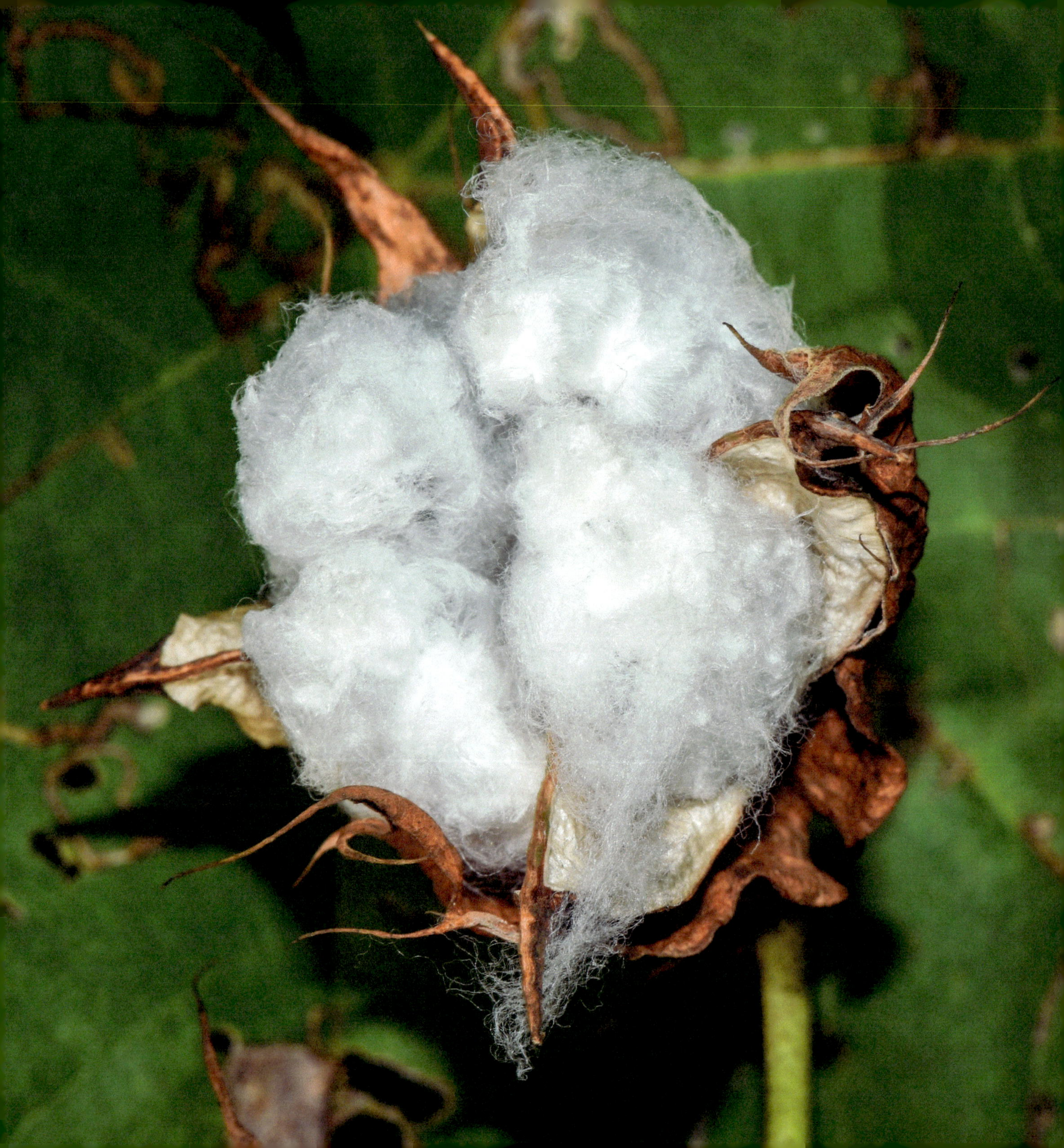

Part Four: Plants and Traditions on St. Martin

RICE AND PEAS
A classic Caribbean combination

The combination of rice and peas or beans is loved all over the Caribbean, and has many variations. What are the roots of rice and peas on St. Martin, and why is this dish so popular?

In St. Martin and the Eastern Caribbean, the Pigeon Pea (*Cajanus cajan*) is typically used in this dish. It was brought to the Caribbean from Africa, and grows well here. It can survive the dry season and produces lots of food with little care. It's still grown today in backyards all over St. Martin.

Rice also has a long history in the Caribbean. African Rice (*Oryza glaberrima*) was domesticated in Africa and was brought to the Caribbean by enslaved Africans. But it was not widely grown on St. Martin or nearby small islands. Here, available land and labor were focused on sugarcane, and rice was imported from Africa. Rice was one of few dry provisions able to survive the trip across the Atlantic.

During the 20th century, rice consumption in the region tripled. Perhaps this is because fewer people grew traditional ground provisions like cassava and sweet potatoes. Immigration to St. Martin brought new recipes featuring red beans, black beans and black-eyed peas. But on this multicultural island, rice and peas is a traditional recipe that still satisfies.

The pigeon pea is still grown locally. (Illustration by Harriet Anne Thiselton-Dyer)

Often associated with Asia, rice was also domesticated in Africa.

Rice and peas photo taken by Mark Yokoyama at Yvette's Restaurant in French Quarter.

WORLD FRUITS
Sweet trees from afar

St. Martin has some delicious native fruit trees, but many favorites were brought from other places. The Mango and Pomme Surette come from Asia originally and were brought during the colonial period. Other fruits were probably brought by Amerindian people during prehistoric times, like the Papaya and Kinnip. All of these trees have been part of the local landscape for generations, and their fruit is part of local culture and cuisine.

Mango (*Mangifera indica*) is perhaps the most popular fruit on St. Martin and in the Caribbean. The tree is originally from South Asia. There are many varieties. The "Julie" is one that is particularly popular on St. Martin. Usually mango trees produce a tremendous amount of fruit in early summer. Hurricanes or drought can disrupt this, causing trees to bear fruit at other times or not at all.

Papaya (*Carica papaya*) is grown all over St. Martin. The name "papaya" comes from the Arawak language. The Spanish adopted the word from the Amerindians they met in the Caribbean. Studies show the plant itself is native to Mexico, and was spread by Amerindian peoples during prehistoric times. Today, many enjoy its colorful fruit. Papaya fruit, seeds, leaves and roots are also used in bush medicine, to aid digestion and get rid of worms. (Illustration by Bertha Hoola van Nooten, 1880)

The Kinnip (Melicoccus bijugatus) is a popular fruit on St. Martin. When it's in season, kids sell clusters of these small green fruits on the roadside. Beneath the skin of the kinnip is a thin layer of sweet pulp and a large seed. The kinnip tree is native to South America, and was probably brought to the Caribbean by Amerindians during prehistoric times. (Illustration by Étienne Denisse, 1846)

The Jujube (Ziziphus mauritiana) has many names, but on St. Martin it is almost always called Pomme Surette, even by English speakers. It is originally from Asia, but has been introduced to many tropical areas. It was probably brought here for its fruit, but its leaves are also used to feed goats and other animals. It sends down deep roots quickly, helping it survive dry conditions. (Illustration by Jean-Théodore Descourtilz, 1827)

Mango

SEEDS OF TRADITION
The deep connections of African plants

African plants on St. Martin often have uses, traditions and folklore connections that stretch all the way back to Africa. And because humans evolved in Africa, the plant traditions on that continent are the oldest in the world. While many of these plants have gained new uses and meanings in the Caribbean, they are also a powerful link to to African heritage for many Caribbean people today.

The Baobab (Adansonia digitata) is an iconic African tree. It has many uses: its leaves, fruit and seeds are edible. It is also part of legends and myths in many African cultures. Huge old baobabs on many Caribbean islands suggest the species was brought here by enslaved Africans during the colonial period. On St. Croix and Barbados, there are baobabs with trunks over 15 meters around. On St. Martin, the largest baobab is in Bellevue near the ruins of the St. Jean plantation.

Sorrel (Hibiscus sabdariffa) is native to Africa and Asia, and has been grown for a long time throughout the Caribbean. The outer parts of the flower, called the sepals, swell into a red fruit after flowering. This part is boiled and then cooled to make a drink. The drink is called sorrel, and is often served around Christmas time. Similar drinks are prepared in many African countries, sometimes combined with mint or fruit juice. (Illustration by Lydia Byam, 1800)

Many of the largest trees you see on St. Martin are Tamarind trees (Tamarindus indica). The tamarind is native to Africa, and was brought to the Caribbean hundreds of years ago. It is grown for its fruit and wood, and it's also used in bush medicine. Large tamarind trees in pastures give midday shade to cattle and other livestock. Tamarind trees also help many native animals. The loose bark of large trees offers hiding spaces for geckos, spiders and insects.

Castor Bean (Ricinus communis) plants are a common sight on St. Martin, but this plant is native to Africa and the Middle East. Castor seeds have been found in 4,000 year-old Egyptian tombs. The oil from castor seeds was used for oil lamps, machinery and medicine. Castor oil is still produced on St. Martin today. In addition to oil, the seeds contain a deadly poison called ricin. Castor seeds are beautiful. Each one has a delicate, unique pattern. (Illustration by Marianne North, 1873)

Castor Bean illustration by Basilicus Besler.

YESTERDAY'S HARVEST
Crops grown for export on St. Martin

Colonial agriculture is connected to many of the worst actions in Caribbean history. Amerindian people were killed or forced to leave their islands. Beautiful forests were cut down, sending animals and plants to extinction. Profits came from the brutal enslavement of people. But many of the plants that were part of this terrible history have found new roles in the time since, and most of them can still be seen growing on the island.

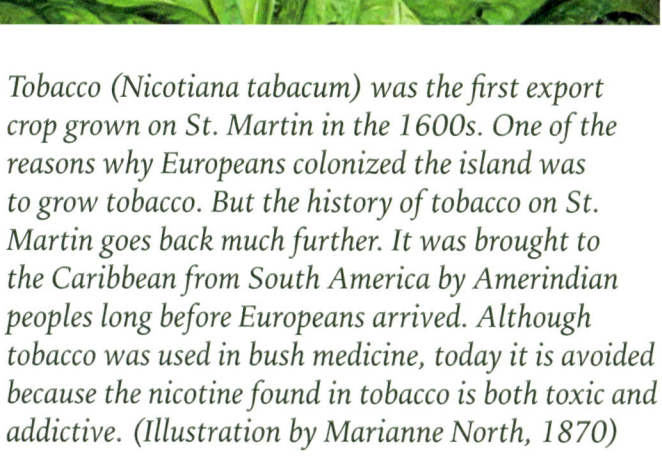

Tobacco (Nicotiana tabacum) was the first export crop grown on St. Martin in the 1600s. One of the reasons why Europeans colonized the island was to grow tobacco. But the history of tobacco on St. Martin goes back much further. It was brought to the Caribbean from South America by Amerindian peoples long before Europeans arrived. Although tobacco was used in bush medicine, today it is avoided because the nicotine found in tobacco is both toxic and addictive. (Illustration by Marianne North, 1870)

Native Cotton (Gossypium sp.) plants grew in the wild on St. Martin before the first people arrived. Cotton was also farmed here. Fields of cotton grew at The Old House in French Quarter in the 1700s. Cotton farming returned briefly in the early 20th century. Sea Island cotton was trendy, and World War I increased cotton prices. In 1922, a cotton-eating caterpillar called the Pink Bollworm arrived and cotton farming ended on St. Martin soon after. It continued on Tintamarre island for another decade.

Coffee (Coffea arabica) was grown as an export crop during the 1700s. It was never the top export crop of St. Martin, and it is unclear how much was produced here. Records show that there were 2,000 coffee plants at Spring Plantation in 1772. Spring is the former name of the estate where The Old House is located in French Quarter. The coffee plant itself is from Ethiopia and perhaps other nearby areas. Coffee is still an important agricultural product on some Caribbean islands, including Cuba, Jamaica and Hispaniola. (Illustration by Étienne Denisse, 1846)

Sugarcane (Saccharum officinarum) is a grass from tropical Asia. It was brought to the Caribbean in 1493, and changed the region over the course of the next 400 years. In the 1700s and 1800s, sugar was produced on St. Martin on several dozen plantations, including The Old House. The sugar industry brought many people to the Caribbean, including enslaved Africans and indentured workers from India and Asia. On St. Martin, almost all forests were cleared to grow sugarcane. (Illustration by Marianne North, 1880)

Indigo (Indigofera suffruticosa)

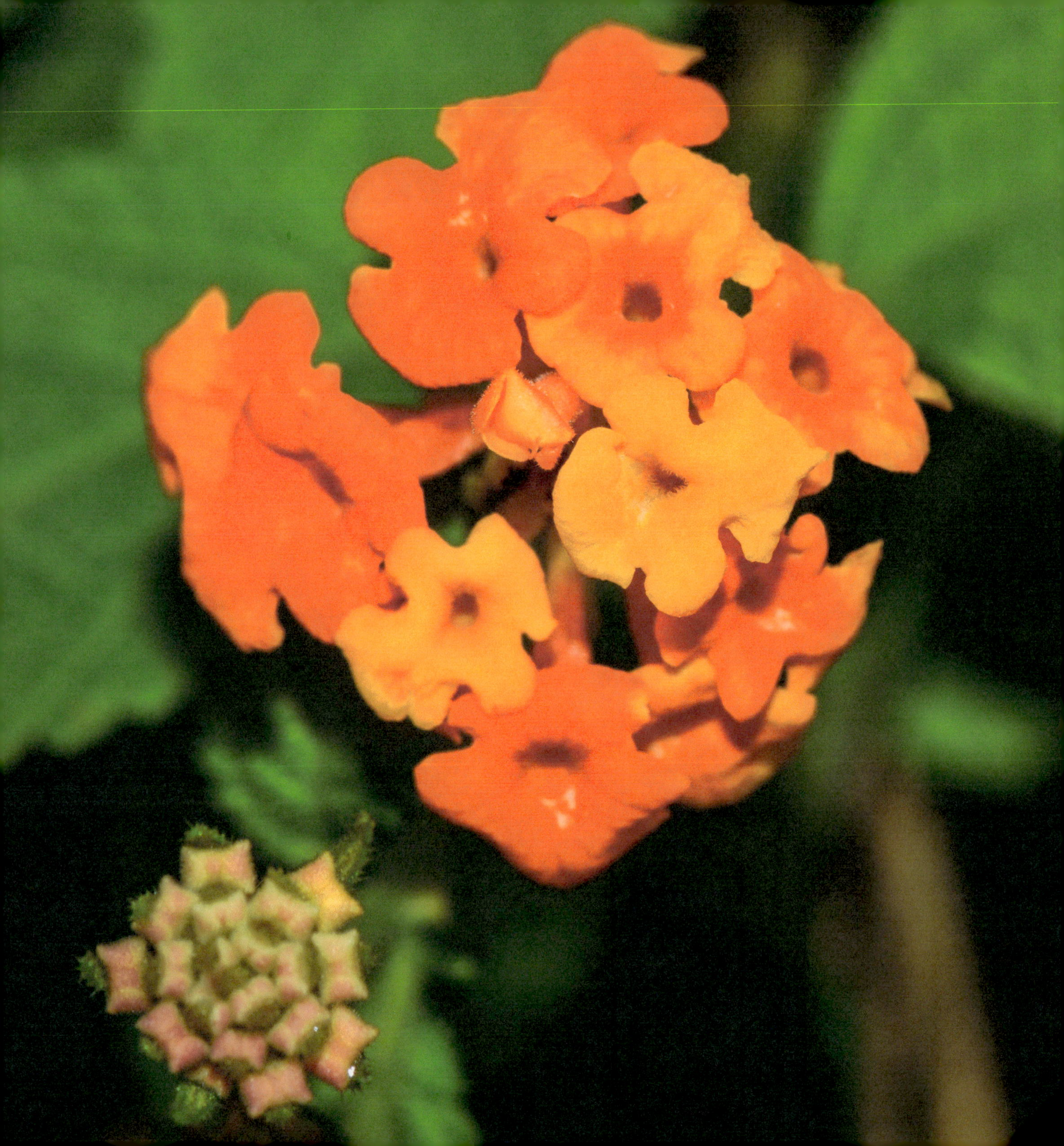

Part Five: Flowers at The Old House

A guide to the flowers of trees and plants at The Old House.

OLD HOUSE FLOWERS

There are hundreds of different plants on St. Martin. Some are native and found only in our part of the Caribbean. Others have been brought from all over the world—as food and medicine, for their beauty or by accident. At The Old House in French Quarter, a historic site where Amuseum Naturalis is located, we have documented over 100 plant species. We have collected images of their flowers here. We have also included some information about the plants and how they are used.

We have divided the plants into groups by their general size and shape, to make this book easy to use. Succulents have fleshy parts that store water. Vines have climbing or spreading stems. Trees are tall woody plants. Shrubs are smaller woody plants. Herbs are smaller plants that don't have woody stems.

Many of the plants in this book were identified by Flora of the Eastern Caribbean Facebook group members, including: Carel de Haseth, Jonas Hochart, Kevel Lindsay, Naqqi Manco and Steve Maldonado Silvestrini.

Above: Waterleaf (left) and West Indian Cherry (right).

Succulents

Succulents are adapted to live in dry areas because they can store water. Cacti are succulents, but there are other kinds of succulents as well. Cacti and succulents are often found where other plants can't survive. On St. Martin, this can be rock walls, cliffs or rocky shorelines. In other areas, it can be harder for succulents to survive because faster-growing plants can grow over them.

Turk's Head Cactus (Melocactus intortus) This native cactus is also known as Barrel Cactus or Pope's head. The "cap" is called a cephalium and that is where the small pink flowers grow. The fruits of this cactus are also small and pink, and they are edible. This cactus is threatened by habitat destruction and animals like goats and donkeys.

Spanish Lady (Opuntia triacantha) This kind of prickly pear cactus is native to St. Martin and nearby areas of the Caribbean. It has many names, including: Jumping Prickly Pear, Jumping Prickly Apple, Raquette Volante, French Prickle, Jumping Cassie, Suckers and Sucking Cassie. Parts of the cactus can become attached to animals or clothing as if they had jumped on.

Aloe Vera (Aloe vera) Aloe vera is originally from the Arabian Peninsula, but it grows well on dry, sunny St. Martin. Aloe was a major export product in Aruba for many years. Small wooden troughs on legs, tilted at one end, were used to collect the aloe sap. Aloe vera is often used to treat sunburn and dry skin. It is also used for many other medicinal purposes.

Vines

Vines send long stems or runners out or up. This allows them to quickly cover large spaces. On the beach, vines like the Beach Morning Glory can spread out over large sandy areas where other plants can't survive. When they do this, they help keep sand from getting washed away by the sea.

Many vines grow on trees, fences and other structures. This lets them reach sunlight without having to grow a thick trunk. Some vines, like Coralita, can cover and smother the plants they grow on.

Vines can be important after hurricanes. Many vines grow faster than trees, quickly providing leaves, flowers and fruits that animals can eat while forests regrow.

Above: Goatbush (left) and Water Lemon (right).

Beach Morning Glory (Ipomoea pes-caprae) This vine is found on beaches and keeps sand from being washed away. It is also known as Goat Vine, Sea Vine, Sea Bean and Patate Bord de Mer. The leaves, roots and seeds of this plant are used medicinally, in particular for stomach and bladder problems.

Obscure Morning Glory (Ipomoea obscura) Native to Africa and Asia, this plant is used medicinally and its leaves are edible.

Rock Rosemary (Distimake quinquefolius) This native vine is also known as Snakevine.

Noyau Vine (Merremia dissecta) This native vine is also known as Bini Bini, Sprain Bush, Saba Spice Bush and Pate d'Amande.

Balloon Vine (Cardiospermum halicacabum) These vines are from the Soapberry family.

Coralita (Antigonon leptopus) This vine is well known for its pink flowers. It is also called Coral Vine, Bee Bush, Cemetery Vine, Mexican Creeper and Zeb Semitye. It is native to Central America and Mexico. In the Caribbean, it is a problem because it can cover and kill native plants. It produces edible tubers underground.

Malabar Spinach (Basella alba) Also known as Spinach Vine, this plant is grown in gardens for its edible leaves.

Goatbush (Stigmaphyllon emarginatum) Also called Wiss, this native vine is common on stone walls and fences.

Maiden Apple (Momordica charantia) This Asian vine has many uses and names, including Cerasee, Lizard Food, Snake Apple Bush, Washer Woman and Bitter Melon.

Burr Gherkin (Cucumis anguria) This spiny cucumber is from Africa, but is also known as West Indian Gherkin, Maroon Cucumber, West Indian Gourd and Wild Cucumber.

Hoopvine (Trichostigma octandrum) This native vine is also known as Hoop Wiss, White Hoop, Liane à Terre and Liane Bawik.

Trinidad Trumpet Vine (Bignonia corymbosa) This non-native vine is grown for its beautiful flowers.

Queen's Wreath (Petrea volubilis) This non-native ornamental vine is also known as Purple Wreath, Lilac and Liane Violette.

Yellow Dad (Cuscuta sp.) These parasitic vines are also known as Yellow Dodder, Yellow Death and Love Vine. Some species are native to St. Martin.

Water Lemon (Passiflora laurifolia) This vine from the passion fruit family has a soft, fuzzy fruit similar to a passion fruit, but much sweeter.

Dutchman's Laudanum (Passiflora rubra) This native plant from the passion fruit family is also known as Snakeberry Vine and Bat Wing.

Trees

Trees are plants that have grown tall to collect sunlight. They have a woody trunk that supports their branches and transports water and nutrients. They usually live a long time.

Trees are important for many reasons. They are big enough to provide shade and shelter. Their deep roots can access water during the dry season when other plants may die. Big trees can produce huge amounts of leaves, flowers and fruit that feed all kinds of animals. Trees on beaches and coastlines help protect the island from erosion.

Humans use trees for shelter, food, wood and medicine. Trees are some of the most important resources on the island. They can also be very beautiful.

Above: Lignum Vitae (left) and Flamboyant (right).

Calabash (Crescentia cujete) This native tree produces a fruit with a hard shell that is used to make bowls and more. The tree is also known as Calebassier, Kalbas and Bowlie.

White Cedar (Tabebuia heterophylla) This native tree grows quickly and was used for timber. It is also known as Cedar, White Wood, Poirier and White Poui.

Lignum Vitae (Guaiacum officinale) This endangered native tree was overharvested for its wood, which is the hardest in the world. It is also known as Gaïac, Palo Santo, Bois Saint and Guayacán.

Sea Grape (Coccoloba uvifera) This tree is one of the most important coastal trees in the Caribbean. Their roots protect beaches from erosion. The trees themselves are popular for the shade and fruit they provide. Each tree is male or female, and only the female trees produce fruit. In the images below, the left shows female flowers and the right shows male flowers.

West Indian Cherry (Malpighia emarginata) Also known as Barbados Cherry and Acerola, this tree is loved for its bright red fruits, which are high in vitamin C.

Flamboyant (Delonix regia) Originally from Madacascar, this tree is grown all over the world for its beautiful flowers. It is also known as the Royal Poinciana, Flame Tree and Flame of the Forest. On St. Martin, it is also known as the July Tree. It is said that branches of blooming Flamboyant were carried by people celebrating emancipation in the Dutch territory in 1863. To this day, it is a national symbol on both sides of the island.

Scarlet Cordia (Cordia sebestena) Native to the American tropics, this tree is also known as Red Cordia and Mapou Rouge. The fruit of this tree are edible, but undesirable.

Tamarind (Tamarindus indica) Also known as the Tamon Tree, this large tree was brought from Africa. It is used to provide shade to livestock and its fruit are used in foods and drinks still enjoyed today.

Cough Bush (Gliricidia sepium) This Central American tree is also known as Rainfall Tree, Quickstick and Glory Cedar. It is used as a remedy for cough and other conditions. Its flowers are edible.

Orchid Tree (Bauhinia variegata) This tree is not related to orchids, but does have a beautiful flower. It is native to Asia and various parts are used in both food and medicine.

Papaya (Carica papaya) *This tree is grown primarily for its fruit, but it also has a wide variety of medicinal uses. It is probably native to Central America, and was likely brought to the Caribbean by Amerindian people.*

Soursop (Annona muricata) *This native fruit is also known as Corossol and Guyabano. It is often used to make juice. The leaves are often used as a tea to improve sleep.*

Sugar Apple (Annona squamosa) *This sweet native fruit is also known as Sweet Sop. Sweet and creamy, it is usually eaten fresh. Various parts of the tree are also used medicinally.*

Cashew (Anacardium occidentale) *This native fruit tree is also called the Cherry Tree, Cherry Nut Tree and Wild Almond. The cashew apple is eaten as a fruit and the seed can be toasted and eaten like a nut.*

Noni (Morinda citrifolia) *Also known as Jumbie Breadfruit, Jumbie Soursop, Dog Dumpling, Pain Killer and Vomit Fruit, this fruit has a strong odor. It is used medicinally.*

Beach Almond (Terminalia catappa) *This non-native tree is known as Indian Almond, Seaside Almond and just Almond. On St. Martin, the almonds are often used to make sugar cakes.*

Cusha (Vachellia sp.) There are several native Acacia trees on St. Martin, also known as Kosha, Cashaw and other similar names. They are used for their wood, resin and tannin.

Tan-tan (Leucaena leucocephala) This Central American tree is also known as Poui Poui, Goat Meat and River Tamarind. It grows quickly and was used to restore nitrogen to soil between other crops.

Chaste Tree (Vitex agnus-castus) Native to the Mediterranean area, this tree has beautiful flowers and a pleasant smell. It is used medicinally, and was once believed to be an anaphrodesiac, hence the name.

Mango (Mangifera indica) This Asian fruit is tremendously popular on St. Martin and worldwide. A number of different varieties are grown. Usually fruit are produced in the late spring and early summer.

White Willow (Quadrella indica) This native tree, and its close relative the Jamaican Caper, are well adapted to the dry climate and can survive in sunny coastal areas.

Rat Apple (Morisonia americana) Also known as Dog Sapodilla, Jumbie Sapodilla and Wild Mesple, this native tree produces a fruit that looks like a sapodilla, but does not taste good.

Barberry (Erythroxylum brevipes) This tree is a native plant from the coca family that produces small, oblong berries.

Clammy Cherry (Cordia obliqua) Also known as Sticky Cherry and White Manjack, this non-native tree bears small fruit with very sticky juice that is sometimes used as glue.

Five Fingers (Randia aculeata) Also called White Indigo Berry, Ink Berry, Fishing Rod and Christmas Tree. Its berries are used as a dye, and it was used as a Christmas tree, staying green for weeks when cut.

Kinip (Melicoccus bijugatus) Selling these fruits on the roadside was a first business for many kids growing up on St. Martin. This South American tree is also known as Spanish Lime, Quenette, Genip, Chenet and many other names. Each tree is usually male or female, but some can be both. Below, the female flower is seen on the left and the male flower on the right.

Shrubs

The St. Martin landscape is covered in shrubs, also known as bushes. In coastal areas, shrubs can often grow where tall trees can't handle the strong wind. In areas that were once farms or pastures, shrubs gradually take over grassy areas. On roadsides, shrubs grow up quickly and get cut down. Shrubs are used in landscaping because their size can be managed.

Because they don't grow tall like trees, shrubs are often dense so they can capture as much light as possible to grow. This can also help them conserve water during the dry season. While grasses and smaller plants may die during the dry season each year, shrubs may drop their leaves to save water and then regrow them when rains return.

Above: Yellow Sage (left) and Bottle Brush (right).

Cotton (Gossypium hirsutum) There are several species of cotton, including kinds that are native to St. Martin. It has been grown for export on the island at various times in history.

West Indian Indigo (Indigofera suffruticosa) This low-growing native shrub was cultivated to produce blue dye. Today it is often seen on roadsides.

Castor Bean (Ricinus communis) This African plant has been grown for its beans for millenia. Castor beans have been found in ancient Egyptian tombs. The beans are used to make castor oil.

Yellow Sage (Lantana camara) Yellow Sage is the national flower of the country Sint Maarten. This plant has been used in many ways. Its leaves are used as tea and ripe fruits may be eaten (though unripe fruits may be toxic). The roots, flowers and essential oil of this shrub are used medicinally.

Lantana (Lantana camara) The same species as Yellow Sage, this plant is also called Wild Sage and West Indian Lantana.

Wild Tea (Capraria biflora) Also called Goatweed, this native plant is used in traditional medicine, often as a tea. It grows well in dry places.

Sweet Sage (Lippia alba) With a sweet and lemony scent, this plant is a bush tea favorite. The essential oil of this plant features many aromatic compounds, and the exact mix varies from plant to plant.

Bitter Berry (Solanum bahamense) Commonly called Canker Berry, Gut Apple or Bahama Nightshade, this plant is used to treat sore throat and thrush.

Candlebush (Senna alata) Also known as King of the Forest and Christmas Candle, this plant is often used to treat skin conditions and contains antifungal compounds.

Monkey Tamarind (Senna bicapsularis) Also known as Black Dog Bush and Money Bush, this plant is used similarly to Candlebush. The flesh of its seed pods can be eaten as well.

Pigeon Pea (Cajanus cajan) Originally from Asia and brought to the Caribbean from Africa, the Pigeon Pea is a popular crop. It can have yellow or red flowers.

Bread 'n Cheese (Pithecellobium unguis-cati) This thorny bush is also known as Cat's Claw. A native plant, it grows well in dry areas.

Milk Tree (Rauvolfia viridis) This native bush is also known as Milkbush, Sassafras and Bellyache Bush.

Wild Guava (Samyda dodecandra) Several different plants are called Wild Guava. This species is not closely related to guava.

Wooly Booger (Corchorus hirsutus) This native plant is usually found in dry coastal areas. In some places it is used to treat cold and flu. Also known as Jack Switch.

Bottle Brush (Cynophalla flexuosa) Also known as Limber Caper and Bayleaf Caper Tree, this bush can sprawl like a vine. It has beautiful flowers with very long stamens.

Tropical Black Sage (Varronia curassavica) Leaves of this plant have been used in a variety of antifungal and anti-inflamatory preparations.

Goat bush (Volkameria aculeata) Also known as Prayer Berry and Privy Hedge, this native plant is sometimes grown as a hedge.

Bellyache Bush (Jatropha gossypiifolia) This native bush is also known as Physic Nut. It grows wild in pastures and other open areas. It has been used to treat a wide variety of conditions.

Teabush (Melochia tomentosa) This native bush is also known as Balsam, Pyramid Bush and Black Widow. It is often found in dry, sunny areas.

Beach Lavender (Tournefortia gnaphalodes) This fragrant native bush is usually found in coastal areas. It is also known as Sea Purslane.

Oleander di Bonaire (Plumeria pudica) This variety of oleander may have been brought from Bonaire. It is native to Central and South America and grown as an ornamental plant on St. Martin.

Devil Weed (Chromolaena odorata) Also known as Baby Bush and Christmas Bush, this plant is popular with butterflies because it produces many flowers.

Pride of Barbados (Caesalpinia pulcherrima) Usually considered an exotic plant in the West Indies, it is widely grown ornamentally for its beautiful flowers. It has many other names, including Little Flamboyant, Spanish Carnation, Flower Pride and Peacock Flower. During the colonial era, this plant was used by enslaved Amerindians and Africans to induce abortion to avoid bringing children into enslavement.

Lady's Slipper (Euphorbia tithymaloides) Also known as Redbird Flower and Slipper Spurge, this non-native plant is grown ornamentally on St. Martin.

Apple of Sodom (Calotropis procera) This non-native plant is from the milkweed family and is a host plant for the Monarch butterfly caterpillar.

Bougainvillea (Bougainvillea glabra) Also known as Paperflower, this South American plant is widely grown for its colorful flowers.

Herbs

In cooking, we use herbs to flavor foods. But when we are grouping plants by shape and size, we use the word *herb* for all the smaller plants around us. Herbs are smaller than a bush or tree and don't get woody. Many of them are annual plants: they grow from seed and die within a year. In colder areas, these plants grow in the spring and summer, then die in the winter. On St. Martin, many of them grow during the rainy season and die out during the dry spring.

Herbs have all kinds of uses. Many are edible. Some herbs are grown simply for their beautiful flowers. Others are used in medicinal traditions that go back thousands of years. On St. Martin, bush teas are made from a variety of plants, including herbs. People drink them for general health and to treat special conditions.

Above: Yellow Rain Lily (left) and Chinese Lantern (right).

Vervain (Stachytarpheta jamaicensis) Also known as Blue Flower, this native plant is used to treat high blood pressure, colds and a variety of other conditions.

Stinging Thyme (Plectranthus amboinicus) Also known as Big Leaf Thyme and Jumbie Sticky Thyme, this African plant is a popular herb for seasoning fish and other foods.

Tulsi (Ocimum tenuiflorum) Also known as Holy Basil, this relative of basil is used as a tea, and a medicine. It is also part of some Hindu religious traditions.

Seed Under the Leaf (Phyllanthus amarus) The flowers and seeds of this native plant appear under its leaves. It is used to treat cough, fever and other maladies.

Shining Bush (Peperomia pellucida) This low-growing plant is also known as Rat Ears and Watercress. It can be eaten as salad, and it is used medicinally for eye infection and other conditions.

Basil (Ocimum basilicum) Basil is used worldwide as a spice. In the Caribbean it is also used in bush tea.

Yellow Rain Lily (Zephyranthes citrina) Native to Mexico, this small flower often sprouts and blooms when the first rains arrive after the spring dry season.

Peppermint Lily (Crinum zeylanicum) These non-native lilies are grown as ornamentals.

Man Better Man (Achyranthes aspera) Also called Devil's Horse Whip, the seeds of this plant stick to legs and clothing. It is not native to the Caribbean.

Indian Nettle (Acalypha indica) This non-native plant grows quickly in open areas. The roots affect cats similarly to catnip.

Jumbie Basil (Rivina humilis) This native plant is also known as Blood Berry and Cat's Blood. It has bright red berries which are sometimes used as a dye.

Woodland False Buttonweed (Spermacoce remota) This native plant tends to be found in open areas and roadsides.

Waterleaf (Talinum fruticosum) This native plant is also known as Florida Spinach, Suriname Purslane, Potherb Fameflower and Sweetheart. The leaves are edible and high in vitamins A and C. However, it is also high in oxalic acid, so it should be avoided by some people. The flowers may be pink, peach or yellow.

Chinese Violet (Asystasia gangetica) This non-native plant is grown as an ornamental ground cover. It flowers in a variety of colors. The large flowers are popular with carpenter bees and other insects.

Chinese Lantern (Physalis angulata) Also called Cutleaf Ground Cherry, this plant has edible fruit inside a poisonous paper-like covering.

Tickweed (Arivela viscosa) This non-native plant is also known as Asian Spider Flower.

False Mallow (Malvastrum sp.) Probably one of several similar-looking native species.

Indian Mallow (Pseudabutilon umbellatum) A native plant found in open areas.

Caribbean Caltrop (Kallstroemia pubescens) A native plant sometimes called False Purslane.

Big Caltrop (Kallstroemia maxima) Another native caltrop.

Purslane (Portulaca oleracea) This native plant grows wild on St. Martin and can be eaten as a salad.

Mauve (Melochia pyramidata) A native plant also known as Smooth Melochia and Pyramid Flower.

Bell Weed (Ruellia prostrata) Native to Africa and Asia, this plant grows low to the ground and has light purple flowers.

Tobacco (Nicotiana tabacum) Introduced to the Caribbean, tobacco was the first major cash crop on St. Martin. The plant still grows wild on the island today.

Twelve O'Clock Weed (Sida ciliaris) This native plant is also known as Bracted Sida.

White Jingle Weed (Sida abutilifolia) This native plant is also known as Creeping Sida.

Spanish Needle (Bidens alba var. radiata) Also called Butterfly Needles, this native plant produces lots of nectar for insects.

Periwinkle (Catharanthus roseus) Also known as Old Maid and Bright Eyes, this plant is from Madagascar, but is grown for its flowers in gardens around the world.

Hogweed (Boerhavia coccinea) This native plant is also known as Scarlet Spiderling. It spreads quickly across bare ground.

Little Ironweed (Cyanthillium cinereum) This non-native plant has been used to treat many things, from fever to scorpion stings.

Phasey Bean (Macroptilium lathyroides) This wild native bean is edible.

Rattlepod (Crotalaria sp.) There are many varieties of Crotalaria, and most come from Africa. Some species are edible and others are poisonous.

Caribbean Stylo (Stylosanthes hamata) This non-native plant is also known as Cheesy Toes, Sweet Weed and Pencil Flower.

Hog Purslane (Trianthema portulacastrum) This native plant looks similar to Purslane. It is sometimes eaten or used for medicinal purposes.

Old Lady Coat Tail (Priva lappulacea) This native plant is used to treat sores and sore throat.

Doctorbush (Plumbago zeylanica) This non-native plant is also known as Leadwort and it has been used medicinally in many ways.

Guinea Henweed (Petiveria alliacea) A native plant also known as Conga Root and Garlic Weed.

Baby's Breath Euphorbia (Euphorbia hypericifolia) This native plant is reputed to have medicinal properties. It is sometimes called Chik Weed and used to treat Chikungunya.

Scorpion Tail (Heliotropium angiospermum) A native plant also known as Dog's Tail, Rooster Comb and Bright Eye Bush. Used for pink eye, sores, itches and stings.

This book was developed as a companion to Amuseum Naturalis, St. Martin's free museum of nature, heritage and culture. The Amuseum, and this book, were created by Les Fruits de Mer.

Les Fruits de Mer is a non-profit association based in St. Martin whose core mission is to raise awareness about nature, culture, and heritage. The organization carries out this mission through a free museum, publications, films, and public events. Learn more at lesfruitsdemer.com and amuseumnaturalis.com.

Made with the support from:

Saint-Martin
Caraïbe Française   French Caribbean

RÉPUBLIQUE FRANÇAISE
Liberté
Égalité
Fraternité

AGENCE NATIONALE DE LA COHÉSION DES TERRITOIRES

Made in the USA
Columbia, SC
09 February 2025